Of Aztecs and Conquistadors

Of Aztecs and Conquistadors

The Poetry of

Juan Pablo Jalisco

Juan Pablo Jalisco

I am Juan Pablo Jalisco, poet! I see myself as nothing more nor less than that brief description, though some elaboration is perhaps necessary. I am a man in love, though my passions are divided into three distinct categories, best described as love of family and friends, love of the world around me, and love of all things Mexican! Poetry is my life and soul, and enables and empowers me to explore and examine new thoughts and ideas, and share them with my readers and fellow poets.

Words have always been important to me. Indeed my first experience of seeing my name in print was in a book produced by my local education department when I was just six years old! (The highly imaginative title of that piece was 'My Story"). For as long as I can remember I have written poetry for my family and friends, perhaps for special occasions, or just to entertain them. I love to observe the world around me, to take pleasure from the thrill of tasting new experiences, and then being able to transpose them into words to communicate those experiences to others. I love to explore the interaction between man and nature, and try to ensure that my work always pays due respect to all the diverse creatures who share this planet with us. There is so much to see, yet we are here for such a finite time; it is a great pity that so many of us observe, but do not really see, all the wonders that the world has to offer.

This is the inspiration for much of my poetry, closely aligned with my desire to express my feelings for those closest to me in a format that will long outlive my mortal self. Family and friends are so important; we often don't appreciate their contribution to our lives until it is too late to tell them what they mean to us. Poetry serves to help redress that communication void, and I am proud that many of my works have been published on both sides of the Atlantic. I am also involved in performance poetry, and am part of the production team of the Doncaster Poets Guild's 'Theatre of Verse', which presents poetry to the public in a theatrical setting, in an attempt to bring poetry to a wider audience than normally achieved.

I hope that my poetry also gives the reader a picture of the beauty that is Mexico! A country far larger than I think most people appreciate, its mountains, deserts, forests and beaches, together with its history and sheer cultural diversity, are a never-ending source of inspiration to me. It is a vibrant land, and I try to bring that vitality to the reader in my work.

Finally, I am so proud that since the publication of the first edition of this collection, I was the winner of The Preditors & Editors 'BEST POET, 2008 Award, an award voted for solely by public vote, a wonderful accolade for any writer. My thanks go to all who voted for me and who continue to read and enjoy my poetry.

I am Juan Pablo Jalisco, poet!

Introduction

With all my heart, I welcome you to this short collection my works. Many of the poems in this booklet celebrate the land of magic and beauty that is Mexico! A country of contrasts, from volcanoes and mountains to rain forests and deserts, Mexico is a source of surprise and delight to those who visit its shores for the first time. The words of a humble poet are barely able to begin to describe this land of ancient civilizations and diverse peoples, yet I am foolish enough to try! How many people, I wonder, are aware that long before the major capital cities of Europe had even begun to evolve into settlements, the ancient civilizations of the Olmec and Toltec lived in vast stone-built cities, with paved cities, street cleaners, and even public toilets. By comparison with these people, the Aztecs are quite a modern phenomenon in Mexican history.

Poetry is my life, and I hope here to share with you a little of my passion for the written word. To tell a story in verse in the space of a page or two I have always found to be far more challenging and satisfying than using page after page and relating a tale in essay fashion. This way, the writer is forced to develop the story, reach the middle and then the conclusion, in a very short space of time, without losing any of the essence of the tale. I hope that I succeed from time to time.

Finally, I hope that you will enjoy my humble offering.

Juan Pablo Jalisco

Contents

Amigos Para Siempre

(Friends for Life)

We swim in perfect synchronicity against the rising
tide of lesser relationships,
Rising through the swamp of failed marriages, and
incompatible liaisons, and we hold fast together.
Years may not diminish the steel that bonds our
ties, nor anger blind the roots that bind us tight.
For we share the incomparable delight of that most
rare and precious gift, true friendship.
No judgement placed upon the other, no critical
lament on failures, we give and take,
We encourage, strengthen, commiserate, but always, as individuals, are nothing more than our-
selves.

And though we may be blown upon life's storm-tossed sea, we are each other's sanctuary,
A place to run, a bolt-hole from humanity's inhumanities.
And when the day is over, when the wind howls at the door,
What is there more than the warmth we share to soothe and calm the mind?
How many years have you been here, how many more will we share?
And when one is no more, so shall the other remember, Amigos para siempre, friends for life!

Mexico

(Cancion de las Aztecas, los ninos del Sol)

We are the children of the Sun, we are forever young.
For all time, in perpetuum our song of life is sung.
We live beneath the soothing mantle of the canopy of the sky,
And high above we watch the swirling condors fly.
Rich green forests, golden shores, washed by the crystal sea.
All these things and more, we owe it all to thee.
You govern wind and tide, and rain, then retire to sleep each night,
Your Queen, the moon stands sentinel, bathed in the wash of your light.

You drive the rain that washes earth, constantly refreshing,
Bringing life to all we plant, our corn is ripe for threshing.
The crystal waters of the oceans kiss our golden shores,
And high above us stand the mountains, where the mighty eagle soars.
All these things stand here beneath the mighty Sun above,
Here we live, we dream, we dwell, basking in the warmth we love.
From Chetumal to Ensenada, Matamoros to Volcan,
Dwell the children of the Sun God, here in the land of Man.

Our rivers run their twisting courses, slowly to the sea,
We harvest from them fish to eat, then sing our prayers to thee.
The lush and verdant hillsides of our green and sun-kissed land,
Are home to trees of fruit, and vines tended with loving hand.
Always we remember how these bounties came to be,
Always will we live here in the land of tranquility.
We are the children of the Sun, we are forever young,
For all time, in perpetuum, our song of life is sung. . .

Dia De Los Muertos

(Festival of the Day of the Dead)

Each year on 1st and 2nd November, on the island of Janitzio which stands on Lake Patzcuaro in Mexico, the lives of the departed are celebrated in a unique fashion.

The flames of hand-held torches cast their fingers of fire into the night,
'Tis the time to honour the departed, and, in the evening's fading light,
The procession makes its way to the place of the graves,
Mirrored in the lake's gentle evening waves.

Dressed in finery, laden with gifts, they continue their reverential parade,
To the place of the dead, where sleep the old ones, and here will be pilgrimage made.
Gifts of food and flowers are laid upon the last resting places
Of the dearly departed, family, friends, pictures laid of remembered faces.

All through the night the sound of prayer is heard upon the breeze,
The sound of hymns fills the air, from the penitent, upon their knees.
The words of the Mass drift through the air, touching heart and mind,
The vigil continues 'til dawn's early light, and a new day is designed.

Music accompanies the faithful as they return to the village by day,
Then, as evening approaches the torches are lit, and they slowly make their way
To the little churchyard, and there once again the Dia de Los Muertos revives,
Voices in praise and in prayer fill the air, and so the tradition survives.

The tourists arrive each year in their droves to witness this pageant of reverence
Do they I wonder feel touched by the sight, by this festival of remembrance?
Or perhaps they see Janitzio as being a place out of time,
A curiosity lost in it's cultural past, this island home of mine.

But the world of the city is far away, here life is slower, the air is clean,
And the blessings of God's great creation are all around us to be seen.
So each year we pay homage and deference to the names of those gone before,
We thank God for their lives, and by the flickering torchlight, we offer our prayers, upon the lake shore.

La Puesta Del Sol

(Sunset)

Fading fingers of skeletal daylight reluctantly let slip
The dying embers of a swiftly setting sun.
And the evening prepares to pay homage to the
moon.

A warm and gentle soporific zephyr softly com-
munes
With the sleepy, swaying branches of the serenely
sighing trees,
And the sun sinks ever nearer to the purple-black
horizon.

The fading light is fast-filled with the rush of beating wings
As the birds of the day return to night-time roosts,
They land on branch and twig, and chatter quietly
in reminiscence of the day.

Twilight shadows lengthen, and in the gloaming light
Nature breathes a heavy sigh, and the day retreats,
As all the creatures of the sunlight take refuge from the night.

The ocean swell becomes benign, undulating with a tender rhythm,
Pacific waves play a placid lullaby upon the shoreline,
Their song carried skywards on the breeze.

The last vestiges of eventide are swallowed by the hungry darkness,
The sun gives up its hold upon the day,
And the moon ascends the heavens.

The lunar light casts a pale reflection of the sun on the scene below,
And the quiet hush of night-time exacts its toll upon the day.
The sun has set, the day is done, and tomorrow is yet to be.

Song of Coyoacan

(Within the boundaries of Mexico City stands the ancient Indian city of Coyoacan, which, through the years, has retained its traditional sense of community, and avoided modern-day urban planners)

With rakish verve doth Coyoacan wear its ancient traditions with pride,
Here stands the palace of Hernan Cortes, here did Leon Trotsky once reside.
Writers, artists, and entertainers, give a bohemian air,
To this ancient city within a city, all manner of life is there.
Conchero dancers, elaborately plumed, perform their ancient rites,
And vendors of every imaginable ware, gather here in resplendent sight.
Turkeys and tacos, and spices galore, for sale in the marketplace,

Alfresco theatre blossoms here, in this plaza with its vibrant face.
Once home to Aztec ancestors, now surrounded by modernity,
This enclave is truly Mexico, a true community.
A capital city all around, though here is a beating heart,
Of all that once was long ago, and thus it stands apart.
An enclave of tradition, of values and ancient ways,
Coyoacan stills beats in time, to the rhythm of those far-away days.

Amor, Tierra Y Libertad

(Love, land and liberty)

Amor, tierra y libertad, love, land, and liberty; can man ask for more?
To love and be loved, to share the bounties of the land, and to live free by rule of law.

The love of a man for his fellows, for his family, and for the land on which we live,
Are the foundation stones of prosperity of heart, we can receive only as much as we give.
The land is sacred to our future, we share it with the creatures of nature,
We must preserve the balance, with care and with legislature.
And man has the freedom under the law to exercise the rights of liberty,
What we do with the planet's resources is no-one else's responsibility.

So can we love our planet in the way that we love each other?
Can man really treat each creature on earth as an equal partner, a brother?
Do we treasure the land upon which we dwell, does the earth have faith in man?
Can our laws protect us from our own devastations, if not, then please tell me who can?
For with our freedom to love, our freedom to preserve, comes as well the freedom to despoil,
We pollute the air, we destroy the trees, we poison our life-giving soil.

We strangle the life from the planet, we destroy more than we can create,
And only the future will show the results, for it may be already too late.
The seas are depleted, fish, once plentiful, gone, now at last we attempt preservation,
As the atmosphere thins, the temperature rises, and we attempt a little belated conservation.
Creatures which once roamed free 'cross the earth are now skeletoid museum pieces,
How long I wonder before man himself becomes an endangered species.

Love, land, and liberty, what man can ask for more?
But they mean nothing at all if ignored by a species
that simply shows them the door.

Iguanas in the Evening at Uxmal

The history of the ancients stands silhouetted
against the fading light,
As evening exacts its toll upon the day,
And myriad cicadas serenade the setting sun,
In a scene of ever-changing visual and auditory ca-
cophony.
The colors of the world fade from pastel to dark,
And the great pyramid of the ancients commands
awe in the eye of the beholder.

I sit upon the weathered steps once trod by long-
dead priests and rulers,
Steps saturated by the day-long heat of the once
revered and worshipped sun.
Rising from the jungle, reaching out to touch the
sky,
The stones bear witness to the passage of the past.
The Maya are no longer, their history obscure,
But El Pyramide del Adivino is as real as I.

I close my eyes, and in the gathering gloom,
I can almost hear the sound of warriors in joyful
song,
Of people's voices raised in celebration, when this
was a city of life.
But no, this is just my mind at play, and there, at
the causeway's end,
Rafael Montoya leads his weary mule home for the
night,
Another day of selling souvenirs to the tourists at
an end.

A sudden rush of sound above my head, I look up
and there I see,
A flock of yellow warblers, so many they fill the sky,
as they head towards their roosting trees.
The shadows of the past lengthen, night will soon
be here,
But I am transfixed by my own reverie, as I sit
upon the ancient steps.
As the stones grow cooler, and the sun sinks lower
I sense more than see
Movement all around me, and the steps and stones
become alive.

Iguanas, large and small, converge upon the temple,
And, ignoring me in their single-mindedness, they bypass me without a thought.
I watch, transfixed, as every crack and every niche in every stone is occupied.
And I think that maybe the pyramid is still a place of worship, of a kind.
Sun-worshippers, cold-blooded, in need of the life-sustaining warmth of the mighty sun,
And where better to retreat when the cool of night invades their reptilian world?

The steps and stones on which I sit hold the warmth of the passing sun,
For an iguana in search of a bed, a centrally-heated citadel.
I lose count of their numbers, but watch until the parade is done,
I begin to descend, but as I go, I turn, look back, see a straggler wriggle into a vacant crack.
And as the Pyramid of the Magician stands in silhouette against the moonlight,
I walk slowly home, and my dreams that night are filled with ancient warriors and sleeping iguanas.

The Day the Dancing Ended

(To Maria Conchita Moreno)

Is it true that we have come to live upon the earth?
Are we to live on earth forever?
Only a fleeting moment here!
Even the precious stones crumble,
Even gold cracks and breaks,
Even the shining feathers are torn.
Are we to live on earth forever?
Only a fleeting moment here!

————Aztec poem————

The day the dancing ended, they took your picture down,
No more would you stare down at yourself from billboards all over town
No more for you the whirling skirt, the dazzling twinkling feet,
Just used up posters, so much rubbish, blowing forlornly along the street.

No more for you the sound of applause, the adulation of the crowd,
No more the sound of the music in your ears, always just too loud.
A dancer's time is all too short, upon the stage of life,
And the day the dancing ended cut through you like a knife.

And yet you have many memories, and though they took your picture down,
It seems your face is still well known in many parts of town.
Though you go there very rarely now, the little town of your birth,
Many years have seen you traveling all across this earth.

But the people do remember you, and make you very proud,
Whenever you go home, they gather in a crowd.
They want to talk to the dancing girl who left them all those years ago,
About the places that you've seen, the world they'll never know.

They remind you of the early days, of a little girl who had a dream,
And they make you very grateful for the wondrous sights you've seen.
You have been to many countries, danced in many lands,
But the people here in your hometown still work the land with their hands.

You are always humbled by their reverence, their warmth towards the girl
Who left them all those years ago with her head in a flying whirl.
For you tell them you are no-one special, just a girl with dancing feet,
Whose faded picture on faded paper once blew down this dusty street...

Matador

How old was I when first I saw him? I think maybe four or five,
The old man sitting under the archway, to me he seemed barely alive.
Where the Avenida de los Delfines runs down to meet the sea,
Below the arch on the corner, that's where the man would be.

From beneath his battered old sombrero, he surveyed the world around,
With eyes that looked like tombstones, and he never made a sound.
The birds seemed to know and revere him, they would sit upon his arm,
Sharing with him his meagre food, they seemed to know he meant them no harm.

Yet to me and others of my age, he was a figure to be feared,
We neither knew nor understood him, then came the day he disappeared.
The corner under the archway was suddenly open wide,
As though a void had opened up, because the silent old man had died.

The birds were gone, all was silent, on that corner near the sea,
And, strange to tell, we missed him too, all my little friends and me.
He had been a part of the fabric of our village for so many years,
Now with his passing we seemed to feel the need to shed a few tears.

The day of the funeral came, and much to our surprise
Many people arrived from miles around, to mourn the man with the tombstone eyes.
And as the priest spoke of the old man's life with reverential eloquence
I learned at last that the silent old man had once led a life of consequence.

Many years before my birth he had been a great matador,
Until the day his career died, when the bull had him pinned to the floor.
Upon the horns of the beast he had twisted and writhed in unbelievable pain,
By the time he was free the damage was done, to his body and to his brain.

Never again did Manolito return to the bullring, (for that I learned was his name),
He retired to the village here by the sea, and became a dwindling flame.
Never again would he wear the suit of lights, nor carry his cape of red,
He just stared at the sea, and communed with the birds, his old sombrero upon his head.

The years have flown, and still whenever I pass the archway I can almost see
That broken old man with the tombstone eyes, and I wonder if he ever saw me.
Had I sat with him for a while, had I spoken softly to him, would he even have noticed me
On the corner of the Avenida de los Delfines, where it runs down to meet the sea?

Heroes of the Revolution

(Tierra y libertad!) (Land and freedom!), a slogan
of the Mexican Revolution 1910-1920

In a field upon my grandfather's farm, in a village
I shall not name,
Are the sad and constant reminders of the day the
revolution came.
Seventy five simple wooden crosses, aged and
weathered by the sun
Stand in silent tribute to those who perished by
the gun.
No names adorn these crosses, instead, inscribed
upon each one,
Five words of stark remembrance to, 'A Hero of
the Revolution'.
Were they soldiers of the Government, maybe fol-
lowers of Zapata?
And after all these years have passed, does it really
matter?
For these were men, women and children, the future
of Mexico,
But in this field their futures ended many years ago.

It wasn't a great battle, what happened here did not decide
The course of the revolution, but they were people, and here they died.
Did they fight until the last man fell, believing in their cause,
As many men have fought and died in many other wars?
Here they found their final peace, beneath this dusty earth,
Their names cast upon the wind, over the land of their birth.
My grandfather told me the story of the day the revolution came,
And I shall tell you the tale of those who lie here, buried without a name.
Two small forces met here in the summer of nineteen-fourteen,
Both intent on controlling the village, and the people were caught in between.
In the heat of a murderous crossfire the villagers died one by one,
And the soldiers continued regardless until the battle was won.
As the dust and the smoke of the battle receded, a grim sight was slowly revealed,

Along with the dead of the enemy lay the villagers, in the carnage of that small battlefield.
Their names were unknown to the soldiers, who laid them side by side,
With the fallen combatants of the enemy, also unknown, here, in this field, where they died.
Slowly, new inhabitants came, the village was born again,
But those crosses remind each generation of man's inhumanity to men.
My grandfather was one who came to the village, and found the crosses bare of inscription,
Knowing nothing of those who lay 'neath the ground he sought an apt description.
Then lovingly, and with painstaking care, he set to work with grim resolution,
And that's why each cross came to bear the words, 'A Hero of the Revolution'.

La Bandera

(The Flag)

(Somewhere in Mexico, 1912)

In a village to the East of the mountain Miguel Arconada was laid to rest,
Father Alfonso conducted the mass, and prayed for Miguel to be blessed.
Miguel was a soldier, and upon the casket the flag of the nation was laid,
And prayers were said for his untimely death, for the ultimate sacrifice paid.
There were tears from his mother, his sister, his brother, oh, how they cried,
They cursed the men who lived by the gun, they were the reason Miguel had died!

In a village to the West of the mountain Ramon Torrado was laid to rest,
Father Roberto conducted the mass, and prayed for Ramon to be blessed.
Ramon was a soldier, and upon the casket the flag of the nation was laid,
And prayers were said for his untimely death, for the ultimate sacrifice paid.
There were tears from his mother, his sister, his brother, oh, how they cried,
They cursed the men who lived by the gun, they were the reason Ramon had died!

Like a forest fire for ten long years the hell of the revolution raged,
Death and destruction walked hand in hand, as though the devil had been uncaged.
And all the people who fought in that war, they all believed their cause was right,
So many funerals were held in many villages for those who'd perished in the fight.
And upon the caskets were laid the flag of the nation for which they'd died,
Red, white and green, on caskets all over the land, same flag..., different side!

Maria Conchita Moreno

(dreams can come true)

Maria Conchita Moreno, I loved you when you were a child,
With your dancing eyes, your gleaming smile, and your dark hair, free and wild.
We played the games of our childhood, together always we'd be,
In the garden of my father, I carved our names on a twisted tree.
We walked the banks of Lake Patzcuaro, our footsteps echoed in the sand,
You were my dream of my forever, my heart was in your hand.
So we grew and we blossomed together in the pueblo where we were born,
'Til the day came when manhood meant I must leave, and from my sweet love I was torn.

Maria Conchita Moreno, to Mexico City I had to go,
And alone through the years of study, in my heart
I missed you so.
My letters you answered, every one, by return,
though you were so far away,
But your love lived deep in my beating heart, and
I needed you more with each passing day.
When vacation time came, I journeyed home, long
hours on buses and train,
With a picture of you engraved in my heart, I
couldn't wait to see you again.
The short weeks we would spend together, would
fly by with sadistic haste,
But I promised you always that I'd return, for the
pleasures of love to taste.

Maria Conchita Moreno, at last the day came to pass,
My studies were over, my future assured, and finally, at last,
I returned to the village once more to my love, and fell down upon my knees,
And the child of my youth, the girl, now the woman, heard my voice and answered my pleas.
Though the years have passed, I will never forget the days of our childhood dreams,
When a smiling sun looked down and approved of our love, I see you now, and it seems
Like only yesterday I carved our names on that tree, yet half a century has gone by,
And yes Maria Conchita Moreno, my wife, your smile still makes my heart fly.

The Horizon of my Dreams

(Mexican Memories)

A flaming ball sinks slowly beneath the rooftop
horizon
of this bleak, industrial landscape,
And, though a thing of beauty, peaceful even, in
this evening stillness, it is not the sunset of home.
No gentle waves break upon the sanded shores of
my beautiful bay, no children playing in the quiet
surf.
My mind travels in time and space to that place
across the world where the sun sets as a disappear-
ing fiery orb into the warm tranquility of the calm
Pacific,
And cormorants wheel in silent tribute to the calm
sea breeze,
the warmth of a Mexican evening.
In place of the cormorants I see only the whirling
plume of rising smoke from a factory chimney.
The warmth of this foreign evening is besmirched
by the stale smog of another day of industrial production and pollution.

And yet, I am happy here, I have friends, and a new home,
I am productive in my adopted land, and I am accepted,
Not for what I have, or what I offer, but for myself.
This bleak industrial landscape, this alien, foreign land,
Is home now, with its strange music, customs, and food,
Though I would give much for an enchilada, a taco with the taste of my birth land.
So I close my eyes, and dream, of a sun-kissed bay, of wheeling cormorants,
And of languid clouds hanging over languid hills, lazily rolling down to meet the shore.
The sun takes its leave behind the corrugated factory roof, darkness rushes in to herald the cool of night, Mexico is far away, but I am not sick for my homeland,
For here is home, and my land of long ago is here with me,
Always and forever, indelibly printed in my mind, and I can visit whenever the factory skyline pales into the horizon of my dreams...

The Rythym of Romance

(To Maria-Conchita, who was one of the 'swaying senoritas').

The gentle strains of a romantic guitar drift upon the soft evening breeze,
Swaying senoritas accompany the man with a voice rich enough to stir a thousand hearts,
And as I sit upon the sand, gazing out upon infinity, my soul sighs in deep contentment.
I watch the slow tango of the undulating waves as they reach out to kiss the shore,
And I could swear that they too can hear the music,
That they sway to the rhythm of the sounds of love carried on the evening breeze.
The sunset gathers pace, and the light of day sinks ever faster into the far horizon,
And still the sound of music, the gentle voices of love fill my ears, and touch my soul.
The dying embers of the day look skywards imploringly, the blue of the sky darkens into night.
All around the bay, the lights of evening blink into life, and still I sit upon the sand, content.

With the darkening night the lights of the town reflect and twinkle upon the waves,
Which seem to gently hum in accord with the song of love whose essence drifts slowly out to sea
Sending its message of romance far into the night, into the infinity of the ocean's caress.
I think that perhaps the breeze pays homage to the sound of romance, as it helps it on its way.
The heady scent of orchid, camellia, and gardenia meld together and drifts across the sand,
And the sounds of the passion mingle with the heady perfume of the night.
The lights of a tiny fishing boat in the bay wink a lovers greeting to the lighthouse on the hill,
And, slowly, in unison with the rhythm of romance, my senses are filled to overflowing.
I close my eyes, and am enveloped by the sounds of music, voice, and ocean swell,
By the sweet perfume of evening as it cleaves to the salt-scent of the breeze.
A dazzling moon clutches the night close to her breast, and the shadows of their joining
Fall upon the world below, mirroring the rhythmic rapture of the passion of love's song.
I am surrounded by the warmth of love's own reality,
I am falling for the dream,

Of love, of stories rendered by the unseen voices, the magic of the sound of the single romantic guitar.
I am truly enamoured, I am lost in the night, beguiled by the goddess of the moon,
I have been touched by the sound of love,
And as the singers depart, and the music stops, I rise from the sand,
Walk home with hope in my heart, I am love with the romance of life.

Sleeping Giants in Sunday Best Hats

In the desert of Sonora, in the heat of the afternoon,
I witnessed nature's hand at work, though it was
over much too soon.
In this drought-parched barren landscape, I came
across a giant,
Accompanied by many smaller companions, though
all entirely self-reliant.

For three long years she had stood there, living on
nothing but her reserve,
Now at last the signs were good, maybe a chance
for her future to preserve.
Her skin was dry and hard, and scorched by the
unrelenting heat of the sun,
And the giant waited, patiently, maybe knowing
what was about to come.

A subtle change in the air above, and the sky began to change its hue,
Clouds of white and purplish-black replaced the powder-blue.
Orange-yellow streaks of lightning cut a swathe through the gathering cloud,
And peals of thunder echoed through the sky, growing ever nearer, ever loud.

The cavalry of charging clouds gathered pace in the darkening sky,
Approaching the standing giant, who waited, patiently, and Oh so dry!
A final peal of thunderous rage and the sky was rent as though by the sound,
And a cascade of life-giving rain began to fall on the stony desert ground.

The lightning cut through yet more clouds, ripping holes in the angry sky,
You could almost hear the giant drinking, anxious not to let this chance pass her by.
Before long, with grim predictability, as quick as it came the storm was gone,
And the giant stood there once again in the glare of the afternoon sun.

But now life was different, the rain had rekindled the land,
And the giant, and all those around her, as if aided by some unseen hand,
Sprouted forth upon her head a blossom of the wild,
As though giving birth after all this time to a long-expected child.

A perfectly formed white flower, yellow centered, proudly sat
Upon the top of the forty foot cactus, like a delicate Sunday-best hat.
And all the giant's companions joined in this great parade,
And the desert was filled with nature's colors, Oh what a sight it made!

In too few days the flower was gone, and with it, all the others,
So the giant returned to sleeping in the sun, along with her sisters and brothers.
She would stand in quiet serenity until the time when the thunder would roar,
When the lightning would rend the sky and the rain would bring life to the desert once more.

Teayo, The Dream Catcher

The old man all in white sits beneath the canopy
of the same tree, every day.
So old, he seems like one of the ancients himself,
so old, he is almost timeless.
A once expensive, though well-worn Panama hat,
a gift from a tourist, adorns his head,
From which, steel grey tresses of ever-lengthening
hair cascade over stooped shoulders.
So every day he sits here, el viejo, (the old one),
and every day, the people come.
They come in search of dreams and good fortune,
from this man as old as time,
They seek his wisdom, they beg his knowledge, they
sit quietly before Teayo.
His name, (it is said it means lightning), is older
than time can remember,
And he sits and he listens to each visitor, in a
hushed, patient silence.
From beneath his hat his eyes stare into the other's,
he almost sees their thoughts,
His eyes, as grey as his flowing hair, seem to pen-
etrate the visitor's soul.

No-one speaks, the silence freezes in time, and he slowly reaches out,
He takes the hand of his companion, holds it tightly, shuts his eyes,
And Teayo dreams a silent dream and takes into his heart
The dreams and aspirations of the one sat in his grasp,
He breathes a little quicker, his body seems to float, just above the ground,
Minutes pass in this silent bond, the visitor entranced, until without any warning,
The illusion is broken, his eyes see once more the face before him, and he smiles.
Releasing the hand of the aspirant, he turns slowly to his table,
And his hands move at deceptive pace, he turns back and holds aloft
The prize for which the visitor came, a thing of beauty to behold.
Delicate, and unique, a circle of wood, of bell, and feather
And fine threads, spun from a traveler's thoughts.
For no more than a few pesos, each and every day,
The old man in white sits beneath the tree, the people come, young and old,

He stares into their minds, he holds their future's in his hand,
And he fashions for them, their very own, personal dream catcher.

Juan Pablo and the Dolphin

There are moments when the weight of memory takes me back to the day,
When, in the azure blue Pacific, I joined a dolphin in play.
And of all the memories in all of my life, this is the greatest I can find,
A pinnacle of remembered joy which leaves all others far behind.
I'd seen these wondrous creature in pictures as a child,
Never dreaming I'd ever be so close to one swimming free in the wild.
I joined her in the ocean, just a few feet from the boat,
She approached me very carefully, maybe checking to see if I'd float.
I felt no fear or trepidation as she looked me in the eye,
From no more than two feet away, and so I thought I'd try
To reach out a hand in greeting, to touch this gentle ocean queen,

She was a creature of great beauty, more beautiful than any picture I'd ever seen.
It seemed she had no qualms about my gentle stroking hand,
She seemed in fact more interested in my blue and green headband!
She inspected it quite closely, I took it off and held it out,
And she took it from me gracefully, with the end of her pointed snout.
She tossed it in the air, she swam around it for a while,
Then I was lost in admiration as she returned it with a smile.
I say she smiled, for that's how it looked, she was grinning, I could tell,
And I just knew I'd made a friend of her, as we bobbed in the ocean swell.
Imagine now my wonderment as upon her back she rolled,
I stroked her from her chin to tail, her skin was warm, not cold.
Though not quite as I'd imagined, her flesh was hard and a little rough,
But we continued in our strange cotillion until she decided she'd had enough.

She righted her sleek body, and I seized upon the chance,
Gently caught her by one flipper, and so began an oceanic dance.
She swam in ever growing circles, with me clinging to her side,
In graceful partnership we moved, through the waves we seemed to glide.
I felt the sense of power as she moved with supple grace,
As I held tight to my new found friend I turned to look her in the face.
Her left eye was looking back at me, she seemed to sense my pure elation,
And I'm sure my dolphin winked at me, and I was awed by the sensation.
She swam close to the boat, and came to a halt, and we bobbed together in the sea,
I felt that we were truly friends, my Pacific dolphin and me.
Now she clicked to me in her dolphin tongue, the message I couldn't tell,
I think she was saying good-bye to me, so I said good-bye to her as well.
She allowed me to kiss her on the head, a final 'click', and she turned away,

And I shall live with the memory all of my life, of me and a dolphin at play!

Hummingbird

Beneath the spreading mantle of an ageing cypress
tree
I sat alone in quiet contemplation.
The not-too distant sound of waves softly breaking
on the beach
Added peace to my mood of reflective meditation.
The sky above was clear and blue,
As blue as the nearby sea.
The air was filled with an air of calm,
I felt surrounded by tranquility.
I sensed a movement not far away,
I looked and listened and then I heard,
The beating of the throbbing wings,
Of a feeding hummingbird.
He was hovering quite close to me,
Oblivious to my presence.

Intent upon the task in hand,
Seeking the flower's essence.
A gourmet meal of nectar, for this flying connoisseur,
Was all that captivated him, and I watched him as though in a trance.
So small and yet so beautiful, with his throat of ruby red,
His long beak stabbing back and forth, in a sort of aerial dance.
His tiny wings moved swiftly, they were nothing but a blur,
Like an aerial dart, the hummingbird gradually took his fill.
Then suddenly, the bird was gone, as suddenly as he'd arrived,
With speed that much belied his size he flew, and once again all around me was still.
I was moved to think of the little bird, and his display of in-flight refueling,
As I sat and resumed my afternoon of quiet contemplation,
For it had been a privilege, to witness one of nature's wonders.
To watch the hummingbird, so close at hand, take his afternoon's libation.

Where Dolphins Play

There are no horizons in this world,
Just an ever changing vista of wonderment,
Of new discoveries to be made.
Sunlight casts a gleam upon the azure waters
of a softly undulating ocean, and here,
Dolphins play.
Within the sight of distant shores,
Leaping in aquabatic formation,
Free beyond our wildest dreams,
At home above and below the waves.
Their voices call in exultation of the sheer joy of life.
Here, far from Man's abode,
'Neath warm, cloudless skies.
Riding atop the wave crests,
Playing games amidst the surf,
Liberated from the static shore,
Here, dolphins play. . .

The Birth of Paricutin

(In 1943, the village of San Juan Parangaricuto in the Mexican state of Michoacan was slowly destroyed by the eruption of a new volcano, Paricutin, which began in a peaceful cornfield on a warm summer's day).

Devastation and beauty walked hand in hand, they had a union to consummate,
The families of San Juan walked hand in hand to church, their daily mass to celebrate.
In the fields around the village, all was quiet, all was still,
The only movement to be seen, a condor circling a distant hill.
As the sun rose ever higher, as the warmth of day grew with the passing morn,
So devastation and beauty lay together, and their awesome offspring was born.
In the subterranean depths of the womb-like cornfield, a rumbling sound was heard,
And as one, the villagers moved en-masse, to see why the peace of the day was disturbed.

There, in the centre of the crop of life, was a fiery, roaring cone,
The people huddled together, yet each felt strangely alone.
The sound grew ever louder, the cone spread out across the land
And day by day a mountain arose, and the people tried to understand,
What power had sent this curse upon them, as higher and higher it rose.
And the fires grew ever hotter, burning ash assaulted eyes and nose.
Lava spewed forth from the hole, the terrible sound filled the ears,
And the people of San Juan began to leave, in fear, and in tears.
One hundred meters, then two then three, ever growing, wider, higher,
Devastation beyond their communal knowledge, a nightmare of lava and fire.
Yet midst the devastation, there was a beauty to be seen,
Primeval in intensity, as the birth of the sun must have been.
The rising torrent of sulphorous ash and gas, and molten lava spread it's tentacles until,

Smothered by its fiery birth, San Juan lay quiet
and still.
Thus was born Paricutin, in the province of Michoacan,
And thus died San Juan Parangaricutiro, now deserted, to a man.
Yet, to this day, half-buried in the lava field, the
remains of the church stand out proud,
Its spire pointing at Heaven above, from within it's
solidified shroud.
Though no-one has lived there for many a year, the
house of God stands sentinel,
Over the birthplace of nature's work, and one can
almost hear the bell,
Tolling in the summer sun, calling the faithful to
prayer,
Where devastation and beauty met, where the people are no longer there.
And one day soon may come the day when Paricutin
will rise again,
And the lava will flow, the spire will fall, and who
will remember then,
That once the corn did gently sway in fields tilled
with loving care,
And people lived and dreamed in this place where
now only tourists come to stare?

They come to see the great volcano, San Juan they do not see,
For San Juan died so long ago, the village just ceased to be.
For when devastation and beauty met, beneath the warmth of that summer sky,
In order for their child to live, poor San Juan had to die. . .

Tomorrow

Autumn leaves fall like showers from tired trees,
As summer is finally brought to its knees.
And birds look skywards singing plaintive pleas.
But tomorrow really is another day.

And will tomorrow bring rewards,
As each of nature's creatures moves towards
Winter's grip, those frosty swords,
But tomorrow really is another day.

Now winter sits heavily on autumn's shoulder,
Winds blow stronger, the air becomes colder,
The icy hand grows inexorably bolder.
But tomorrow really is another day.

Tomorrow, tomorrow, always tomorrow,
The answer always to today's tale of sorrow.
And until then, someone else's hope we'll borrow,
But tomorrow really is another day. . .

Los Arboles En Invierno

(The trees in winter)

They stand in solemn ranks, and look so lonely.
Stripped of covering and dignity, exposed to winters chill,
They point twisted fingers upwards in accusation and in sadness at their annual betrayal.
No voices can they raise, nor revolution can they inspire,
As they stand in solemn ranks, looking lonely.

The snows of winter fall and form white carpets on the ground,
And hang heavy on the naked torsos of the forest.
Rain soaks deep within the cracks exposed by winter's frosts,
And the lonely trees can only shiver where they stand.
In solemn ranks, looking lonely, in silent tears.

The gales blow hard, ice hangs from branches,
Audible cracks herald falling twigs,
Like broken fingers they drop and splinter upon the
frozen ground,
And no-one hears the cries of the mother tree,
For she must stand in solemn silence, oh poor sad
lonely tree!

The Colors of the World

The skies were blue, the grass green, the earth a dusty brown,
At the dawn of the twentieth century, an optimistic sun looked down.
The technology of nations gathered pace, man learned to fly,
But the honeymoon years of the golden age were slipping quickly by.

The skies were smoke grey, the grass was gone, the earth stained bloody red,
As the nations of civilized humanity ignited in war, and counted the countless dead.
The abyss of man-made Armageddon opened its bloodshot eyes,
And in its cold embrace each lost soul in perpetuum now lies.

Not content with nation upon nation, revolutions took their place
In the slaughter of the innocents, in these wars with a civil face.
From the mighty Tsar of the Russian steppes, to the plains of Mexico,
Brother against brother, as the current of blood increased its flow.

And as the world sat back in optimism, as the bloodbath slowed,
So hopeful misplaced belief in 'Peace for our time"
gradually followed.
The appeasers of the tyrants tried at foolish cost,
To stem the tide of yet more death, their cause prematurely lost.

For soon enough the nations of the world found a new excuse,
To show to all their neighbors that peace was of no use.
So the skies were turned to ashen grey, the grass to bloody red,
And the earth just cried its heart out, as man once more set out to count the dead.

So holocaust and atom bomb, and missiles in the sky,
Still couldn't shout the message out, and the innocent still die.
For man has a great propensity to forget the recent past,
And concentrate on the here and now, so no war can ever be the last.

Each altercation between nations, each religious conflagration,
Will only serve the needs of the zealots of any nation.
The words of the peacemakers are lost in the scramble to war,
And the colors of the world may never be in harmony any more.

The Melody of My Heartbeat

Life strums a melancholy guitar melody upon the strings of my heart
As it beats to the ever slowing ballad of my years.
The Latin rhythms of my youth still stir my inner soul,
But now I move to the sounds of the romance of time,
And memories enfold my being.
The heady days of youth are gone, lost forever in the mists of time,
And the soft strains of evening fill my mind, the light of day grows dim.

The melody is there, never changing, just slower than once before,
The melody of exuberance gives way to the melody of ageing peace.
The timing is different that's all, the sound of the tune stays the same,
But now there's a gentle drum beat, deep in my beating breast.
It beats in discord to the melody, I hear and feel its tremulous sound.
And the melody is twisted by the unsynchronized rhythm of the drum.
So when the ballad of the years reaches its final chord
I will listen to the sounds of the angels refrain as they strum their melody on the strings of my heart.

The Night Sleeps Soft

The night sleeps soft upon its bed of cushioned darkness,
And the lights of other worlds are naught but distant dreams.
The gentle cocoon of moon shadow casts its mantle over the remnants of the day.
And silence descends upon all thought.

Hushed and furtive whispers slide past sleeping mountain tops,
And fall to the unseeing ground, unheard by the silence below,
Where shadows, like faceless specters dance through the dark of night,
Their names known only to the wind.

Mirrored lakes and oceans dream in quiet contemplation,
And the constellations of the heavens play upon their waves.
Millions, nay billions of winking eyes look down upon the sight,
And keep quiet sentinel upon the earth, as night sleeps soft upon its cushioned bed of darkness.

A Personal Genesis, A Question of Genetics

In dreams, I tread the boundaries of subconscious reality,
And, in a haze of unbidden confusion, ask the question,
"Who am I?"

The blood of two continents flows through my veins,
Coloring the ocean of my soul,
Aztec and Toltec, conquering Conquistador,
Images which flood my mind, in the half-world of my sleep.
I hang upon the edge of memory, trying to see beyond the veil,
But it hangs there, blurring the images of the dreams.

Memories of ancient rites, of colors and of words,
Words of ancient meanings, languages long-gone,
The sights and scents of a world apart flood my
sleeping thoughts,
They absorb my soul, until I wake, and they are
lost again.
And all the reminiscences of genetic memory cry
out in unison,
"Who am I?"

For I am the sum of many parts, but the past is
indistinct,
Who can separate the bloodlines of a dream?
Conqueror and conquered, two turbulent pasts en-
twined,
Within the seeds laid long ago is the answer to my
question,
So am I the progeny of history, what was the genesis
of my dream?
Am I East or West, am I the New World or the
Old, for my history is both?

In dreams, I hang upon the edge of memory, and almost touch the truth,
But I am many nations, many people, and the dreams are indistinct, the reality obscure,
So will I ever find the answer to my question, "Who am I?"

Peace At Any Price

The specter of history casts shadows on today,
Yet so many fail to see.
"War is never justified," they cry,
They clearly haven't learned from history.

Or have the memories of evil past
Been buried and forgot.
Have the people who protest the war
Never heard of Hitler or Pol Pot?

Would they prefer that we stand back
Do nothing, be passive lambs, ignore the suffering
in other lands?
Think back my friends, to dark days past,
When freedom made a stand.

Though sanity denies the want,
The need or desire for war.
Tyrants do not go away,
Voluntarily or through word of law.

Freedom has a price,
Or would the peaceniks care to try
To live beneath the tyrants yoke,
Then what would be their cry?

Their shouts would be the loudest,
Proclaiming their human rights.
Perhaps then, and only then,
Would they understand the need to fight.

So for now they enjoy the freedom
To march and to protest,
Until perhaps one day long hence,
They'll understand why men must answer free-
dom's test.

Lonely Without You

I close my eyes, lay down my head, but sleep is
not to be.
I am mocked by the shroud of darkness which en-
velopes me.
I lie stiff in expectation for the touch of my absent
queen,
As the moon is chased across the sky by the sun,
as it has always been.
I burn with the heat of fierce desire, with naught
but time to quench the flame,
And my fiercely burning body screams into the
night, a distant name.
At last the mantle of exhaustion falls upon my soul,

And I twist and turn in troubled sleep, and dreams of emptiness take their toll,
Until, with predestined inevitability, the sun chases the moon from the sky,
Instantly alert, I wake with a bodily sigh.
With the consciousness of demi-sleep, I lie rigid until with open eyes,
I stare at the new dawn overhead, as another long night dies.
I turn in false anticipation and there, beside me all I see,
Is the empty space upon the bed, where my absent queen should be...!.

Dame La Mano, Mi Hermano

(Give me your hand, my brother)

Nothing moved me, nothing touched me,
For I was lost in the darkness of despair,
And the weight of life lay heavy on my soul.
The door to the future had slammed shut,
I hung precariously on the precipice of eternal night.
Seeing no tomorrow, I clung to my final memories,
And drifted towards the final curtain.

But from a recess deep within the darkness,
From somewhere I could not see, came a voice,
It called incessantly and would not be ignored.
"Dame la mano, mi hermano", "Give me your hand,
my brother",
Over and over and over again, in soft tones of re-
assurance,
Calling to me, lifting me, pulling me, imploring me.
And I, who was alone, felt the warmth of another's
hand.

Slowly, as I listened to the oft repeated plea,
The darkness receded, the voice never faltered,
And I saw in the distance, a pale yet inviting light.
It entreated me to reach out, to seek its life giving warmth.
Its implied invitation was addictive, it's beckoning irresistible.
And the gentle voice repeated, in a whispered modulation,
"Dame la mano, mi hermano", "Give me your hand, my brother".

The light grew stronger, the memories diminished,
I felt the breath of a new tomorrow surging through my wounded heart.
The load I carried deep within was slowly lifted by the music of life.
As I awoke from the depths of my despair, I sought the face of my redemption,
To touch the hand of the one who saw my pain, but the room was empty.
Yet in my heart, I felt the presence, and in my mind I still heard the voice,
"Dame la mano, mi hermano", "Give me your hand, my brother".

Eagle Wings, Touching the Sky

I have climbed many mountains,
and tried to touch the sky,
But always, in frustration,
I have found the sky too high.
So I am jealous of the eagle,
who looks down upon the world,
From the highest reaches of the sky
he soars on wings unfurled.
From high above he scans the mountains,
he ascends above the cloud,
He touches that which I cannot reach,
he has freedom from the crowd.
Each day he reaches higher
than I can ever dream,
So I hold the mighty eagle
in the highest of esteem.
I am earthbound, I am impotent,
in my quest to touch the sky,
So I wish I was an eagle,
then I'd have wings to fly!

A Curse On Autumn, Winter's Herald

(Many miles from home)

It is Autumn, the fall, in a strange land,
Where the cold breath of morning brings a shiver
To my bones, and fills me with the dread of the
past approaching Winter.

The sun still shines, though rising later,
As if needing to rest, to gather it's remaining
strength
To face the rigors of the rains, the gales, the snows,
the Winter!

In my homeland, the seasons change with little dis-
cernible change,
Yet here, the leaves fall with gathering haste, car-
peting the ground,
They hurry to escape their tenuous hold upon
branches soon to be exposed to Winter.

Winter, always Winter, it hides behind the skirts of Autumn,
I shiver again at the thought of the months to come.
As Autumn moves inexorably towards its darker, colder cousin, Winter.

The warmth of the days grows shorter, the light is fading fast,
The trees grow quieter as the migrating birds depart,
They know they must escape before they are consumed by Winter.

I feel no love for Autumn, just a sadness in my heart
At the passing of the Summer, the demise of the long, warm days.
And I must prepare myself, like the hibernating hedgehog, for the Winter.

So, with grim inevitability, I shiver once again,
Turn on the central heating, raid the wardrobe for warmer clothes,
And curse Autumn for heralding the arrival of the Winter!

Sunset In the Bay of Banderas

(Puerto Vallarta, Mexico)

Softly undulating Pacific rollers broke gently upon
the shore,
Their sound a symphony of evening peace,
The beach of soft, white, sun-kissed sand, deserted,
save for me..
In the evening sky, cormorants wheeled and whirled
in their last display of the day,
Soon to disappear to their night-time's rest.
In the distance, lush green hills appeared to run
down to the sea,
Iguanas, sated from their daytime basking, scurried
off in search of night-time refuge.
Across the bay, the fishermen hove to, and a tran-
quil peace transcended all around.
Far above, though seeming close, the Sun fell lower
and lower,
It seemed to rush to met the ocean, and I sat and
watched, transfixed, as,

Like a giant fiery orange ball descending from the heavens,
Faster and faster it seemed to move, inexorably sinking,
Shadows lengthened and the waters of the bay turned from sun-kissed blue to twilight pewter.
For a few moments, the dying sun's iridescence seemed to fill the sky, obliterating the horizon,
Then ever faster, the mighty orb sank into the far away waves.
'Twas a sunset like no other that I had ever seen,
I sat, in wondrous awe,
And marveled at this sight of grand magnificence.
Here, I was closer to nature's plan than I had ever been,
I sat a little longer, contemplating the sight I'd seen,
And as the evening drew closer to the coming night,
The air still warm, just a hint of sea breeze.
I was content...

Where the Artists Live

(Seeking the Heart of a Nation)

The words of my old teacher inspire me from time
to time,
Whenever I sit to contemplate the composition of
my next rhyme.
"Go," he said, "to Jocotopec, to the place where
the artists live,
Go, and find within yourself what it is that you
can give.
For to find the heart of a nation, you must explore
its very soul,
Feel its throbbing pulse, see through an artists eyes,
and find your own life's role".
So I went to the place of the artists, a place of
charm and tranquility,
And there I explored my own heart and soul, and
discovered creativity.
Amongst the painters, writers, and songsters who
gathered in the town,
I found my life-long love of words, found many ways
to set them down.

I would sit in the shade of an old palm tree, and watch the world go by,
Hear the orchestra on the bandstand, stare up at the clear blue sky.
I watched the coming and going of many people, heard their daily chatter,
And I would write of all I saw and heard, in varied subject matter.
Sunsets bade the cool of evening, and I would sit in a small cafe,
And watch as the moon would take its place 'midst the dying embers of another day.
I watched the painters paint the sunset, and the songsters sang of the night,
And would sit and take in all I saw, and my mind would record the sight.
I remember a day, the sun was high, and I sat beneath the fronds of my palm tree,
I noticed a painter not far away, and realised he was painting me!
For I was a subject as real to him, as the sun, or the moon, or the birds,
He would paint what he saw in his own mind, his personal vision of a man of words.
What more could I do, I sat very still, as he painted the poet in thought,

For it seemed that by now I was known as such, and now I knew what my teacher had taught.
For here in the place of the artists, I discovered the real me,
Not a captain of industry, a politician of note, a simple writer of poetry.
And I was a poet you see, not because I said to the world that I was,
I was a poet because the world saw me that way, and I thanked the painter because
He had looked into my soul, he had reached for my heart, and placed them on canvas in oil.
Not for me fame or fortune, no ordered life, just a future of pleasurable toil.
Finding the words to record all I'd seen, all the images in my mind,
Became my personal Holy grail, never knowing what I'd find.
For every day is a new experience, on the journey on which I travel,
A poet's journey, new words to find, the mysteries of life to unravel.
So I found the heart of a nation, just as my teacher had said,
Not just in the place of the artists, but right here, inside my own head!

For I knew what he meant, when he sent me there, my teacher, so learned and wise,
The nation's heart beats in its people, and I observe them with a poet's eyes.
Like the painter who saw the poet in me so I write of the people I meet,
Poems of tragedy, love, and trivial things, of people just walking down the street.
I try to see beyond the obvious, to strip away the external veneer,
Heart and soul revealed, in the eyes of a nation, all the passion, hatred and fear.
One day perhaps, when I am no longer, someone will read of me,
Or admire a painting, entitled 'Heart of a Nation', of a poet sat under a tree.

Grito De Dolores

(Call of Dolores)

On 15 September 1810, the ringing of the bell of the church of Nuestra Senora de los Dolores in Dolores by it's curate Miguel Hidalgo was the signal for the beginning of what became the Mexican War of Independence against the Spanish occupation. The town is today known as Dolores Hidalgo!

————————-/————————
-

Sunrise, a day much like any before, but unlike any other to come.
The sun crept higher in the azure sky, and the birds of morning sang.
Then the peace of the surrounding land was broken, there began a mournful sound,
As the bell of Dolores Hidalgo rang, and rang, and rang.

"Cry Freedom!" was her message, and the people rose as one,
To shake off the yoke of the occupier, but a long road lay ahead.
Miguel Hidalgo, curate, rang the bell, lit the flame,
Eleven years of bloody strife would pass, freedom's path not so simple to tread.

But on that day when Dolores called, eighty thousand souls took arms,
And followed the standard of freedom, hope burned bright in the people's heart.
The bell rang loud in the morning, sounded liberty's call,
And the strength of the people's will would grow from this simple start.

"Cry Freedom" was the message, in the tolling of that parish bell,
And the land would blaze for years to come in echo of the sound.
Many would fall, there would be many tears, in the cause of the nation's rebirth,
But the cry of Dolores would not be stilled, through the years it would resound.

Autonomy and emancipation of the people rang with sound of Dolores' call,
And the presumption of the oppressor could never again prevail.
The voices of the people reached out in one great choir,
And their belief, their solidarity, ensured they would not fail.

"Cry Freedom" was the message, nothing more or less,
With the peal of a single church bell, came the people's affirmation.
No more the bonds of servitude, of hapless subjugation,
The Call of Dolores heralded the freedom of a nation!

The Clown, The Man, The Tears

I'm the clown, the entertainer, I'm the life and soul
of the show,
I'm the sad reflection of humanity who the audience
don't see or know.
They laugh and cheer at my stage persona, I'm
everybody's friend,
But they don't care who I become when the curtain
falls at the shows end.
I wear the mask of laughter well, for it fits me like
a glove,
And no-one sees the tears of the clown, the clown
crying out for love.
The sounds of the audience have faded, the clown
goes home alone,
And is deafened by the sound of silence as it echoes
through that lonely home.

The ghosts of every lonely hour are resurrected in my mind,
Until each second of time becomes torture of the most exquisite kind.
For though the body cries out for the sweet relief of sleep,
The mind descends instead into an ocean of thoughts so deep
That the night becomes a darkened path strewn with apparitions,
Screaming banshees, forgotten memories, the mind's accusing depositions.
With morning comes the gathering gloom of the day after the show,
The clown looks in the bathroom mirror, today there's no theatre, and so,

He stands bereft of make up, stripped of his stage-worn smile,
He feels the after tensions of the night before, and ponders for a while,
The cruel and twisted version of the false life of the man on stage,
Each show another fiction, each laugh another page
In the book of life, though the jokes on him, so let's all laugh at the clown,
For isn't that what clowns are for? So let's not let him down!
But as each curtain falls the clown, the entertainer, the buffoon, the life and soul,
Goes home alone without his stage self, and lives in his own personal black hole!

Of Aztecs and Conquistadors

(The Aztec people knew themselves as 'The Mexica')

Have you grown weary of your servants?
Are you angry with your servants?
O Giver of Life?

————————Aztec poem————————

On giant ships they came from a land across the sea,
And the people of the Mexica wondered who these men might be.
They rode upon strange beasts, whose coming shook the earth.
And Moctezuma welcomed them, assuming Quetzalcoatl's promised rebirth.
For the Aztec king was mindful of ancient prophecy,
Which told of the return of the ancient God, who would arrive by sea.
Was this the realization of the prophecy, asked the Aztec king?
And if this was Quetzalcoatl, what new wonders would he bring?
But these were no returning deities, and he would soon regret his decision
To welcome these men as ancient Gods, for they had a treacherous mission.
Cortes was not the God of prophecy, he came in search of Aztec Gold,
And soon the Aztec king would know this was not the God of old.

The people of the Mexica gave all they had, and more,
But the greed of the conquistadors led to inevitable war.
Soon the seeds of suspicion grew, and the uneasy peace gave way,
The people of the Mexica sought to drive the invaders away.
But the invaders had the upper hand, their weapons were too strong,
And they joined with the Aztec's enemies, their victory did not take long.
Moctezuma passed unto the heavens, his son died of the Spanish disease,
And those not killed by the invader's swords were brought by smallpox to their knees.
So Cuauhtemoc, the last Aztec emperor, made his final stand,
And was taken prisoner, and ignominiously hanged.
So perished the Aztec empire, though the story is told,
Of how the Spanish were thwarted by the people who hid away all the remaining gold!

So they laid to waste the beauty that had been the Aztec capital city,
And within the walls of Tenochtitlan the invaders showed no pity.
Throughout the lands of the Mexica, the conquistadors waged their war,
Until, in less than two whole years, the Aztec Empire was no more.
Great cities lost, people slain, a thriving civilization gone,
All for the greed of those wanted the metal that shone as the sun.
Many years would pass, many suns would set, until the people rose again,
To drive out the invaders, and become, once more, free men.
Though all that stood, of ancient times were the ruins of the past,
They fought and were victorious, and became a free nation at last.
And for their new-born country they took a name from long ago,
In honour of the long dead Mexica, they called it Mexico!

Alejandro Miguel De La Vega - Mi Amigo

Alejandro, you were my dearest friend, we were as brothers for so long,
And I will always remember the tuneful sound of your voice in song.
I was not yet quite a man when we met, you were older, but not by much,
We talked in the cantina in a small country village, of music, and words and such.
We spoke of many things, you and I, the day that our friendship began,
Through the years we shared many confidences, in the way that only friends can.
Your work took you to far flung destinations, all over the world you flew,
You performed your arias around the globe, and your reputation grew.

You would send me tapes and letters, I would write back, often in verse,
Never did either one of us know that you carried such a curse.
I was to be married, and you, my dear friend, traveled for twenty four hours,
And arrived on the day of the nuptials, loaded down with bouquets of flowers.
Maria Conchita became my wife, she too was captivated by your charms,
And whenever you'd visit she would welcome you with outstretched open arms.
You were part of the family, you were my friend, a brother in all but name,
At the birth of my son, you were over the sea, but never mind, you jumped on a plane.

Again you arrived with presents galore, for the little one, who we named after you,
And you gave him a gift to be placed in trust until the time that he grew.
Then came the day when your mother arrived on my doorstep in the dead of night,
To tell me that my friend Alejandro was ill, her face a heartbreaking sight.
All your life my friend you had carried within the instrument of your own destruction,
And now without warning, your, time had come, you were hit by a massive eruption
Of the latent cells of genetic default, they exploded within your brain,
And you slowly slipped away from life, and for me, things would never be the same.

The world had lost a fine singer, no more would you grace the stage,
Your mother grieved for her beautiful son, snatched away at such a young age.
I sat beside her in grief at your hospital bed, I was there with you at the end,
And I remember the chasm of desolation I felt as I said good-bye to my friend.
Many years have passed since you left us, Maria Conchita are I are still wed,
My son has grown, but still we speak of a friend whose voice I still hear in my head.
The world has changed so very much since those times so long ago,
When a lifetime friendship was born over a couple of drinks, in a cantina in Mexico.

One Dance, One Kiss, and then Forever

Please come, join me in the dance,
Oh pretty señorita with your eyes so blue.
Come, and let me captivate you, let me
take you to a place you've never seen.
I shall look deeply into those azure eyes,
that brought me to your side, smile your smile for
me alone.
Let us move in sensual rhythm, to the music in
your mind.
Be beguiled my lovely, fragile one,
Be mine forever more, please, smile for me again.
Walk by my side forever,
Never leave me, join my eternal soul.

As I saw you walk across the floor,
Your skirt softly rustling, I was enamoured
in a moment, I knew you must be mine.
Now, as I whirl you round the floor,
you are breathless, lost, entranced,
And, as the night grows ever longer, ever darker,
So you are slowly falling under my spell, becoming
mine. . .
Oh, how I love your smile.
And when the moment comes, when the dance it-
self must end,
Let me lead you by the hand, walk with me in the
garden green,
Lean upon my arm, let me be your guide, feel the
pulsing beat of my heart
As we softly entwine in love.
Let me be all that you seek, all you shall ever need,
Let me feel your lips as one with mine,
And as the first kiss beckons us to our destiny.
I shall love you as no other can, come, see the sun
rise in my arms,
When the dance is over, when our lives begin
anew. . .

Los Colores Del Otoño

(The Colors of Autumn)

Beneath the canopy of the Heavens, all things must
change,
And with the fall of Autumn comes nature's time
to re-arrange.
The mighty sun, a little weary from his daily summer dance across the sky,
Rises a little later, and climbs not quite so high.
The warming rays which nourish earth grow ever
weaker by the day,
And Autumn reaches out to the earth, its own symphony to play.

The ocean waves in the crystal bay are no longer quite so blue,
As the sun yawns in its weariness, they assume a darker hue.
The seabirds wheel and whirl, and then are gone in vast formation,
Like pilgrims they must chase the sun in their annual migration.
And from those who stay here all year round there is heard a song of expectation,
As Autumn heralds the coming of Winter's grip of stark privation.

A cascade of wrinkled, dying leaves falls from the branches of trees too tired to care,
As their branches reach skywards imploringly for a warmth no longer there.
So green turns to shades of red, to russet and to brown,
As nature releases the season's growth, and lays its rustling carpet down.
The creatures of the forest prepare quarters for their winter salvation,
Some turn away from the graying world, and descend into hibernation.

The clouds which danced across the sky, are no longer quite so white,
They twist in the ever growing wind, and run away as if in fright.
They are blown into oblivion, but just as quickly are replaced,
By their dark grey rain-filled cousins, by whom they are displaced.
In the season of the dying sun, the earth itself appears to shiver,
White frost fingers reach out, and place a dusting of ice on the mountain river.

The mighty sun climbs ever slower in the graying sky each day,
As the vibrant colors of Autumn mock his efforts in every way.
For even the sun with all its might must bow before the Fall,
And Autumn, with grim rectitude, casts its growing shadows like a shawl.
The blues and greens of summer are soon no more than a distant dream,
King Winter will soon be here again, but for now, we are touched by his queen!

Recuerdo De Mexico

(Souvenir of Mexico)

Palm fronds swayed and bowed in homage to the
gentle warm Pacific breeze,
Beneath the swaying palm lay the tourist, in abso-
lute relaxation.
With a wide-brimmed Panama hat on his head, and
sunglasses over his eyes,
On the beach at Puerto Vallarta, a rich man on his
annual vacation.

Along the wide expanse of sand came a weather-
beaten figure,
The beach-seller, peddling her wares, weighed down
by her battered old suitcase.
She stopped beneath the shade of the palm, and,
began her usual pitch,
"Home-made woodcraft for sale senor", a broad
smile upon her face.

The man raised himself from his recliner, polite interest in his mind,
And fixed on a wooden dolphin, and haggled to bring down the price.
'Too many pesos' the man intoned, 'How much you give?' the woman replied.
And a price was agreed, money changed hands, the deal was done in a trice.

The tourist was happy with the dolphin he bought, impressed with his bartering skill,
And the old beach-seller was glad for she'd earned enough to pay for many a family meal.
So the man on the recliner went home on the plane, with a wooden dolphin in his case,
The old woman's family ate like kings for a month, so I wonder, just who got the best deal?

Yesterday, I Thought of You

(For Maria Conchita)

Yesterday, I thought of you, and I could smell the aroma of your skin in my mind.
Then yesterday blossomed into today, and you were there.
The wind played a discordant harmony with the golden tresses of your hair,
Your hand swept it back into place, only for the breeze to conduct its own symphony once again.
You gave up the struggle, and, though you thought yourself a windswept urchin, you were as a flower swaying gently in the swirling mistral.

Yesterday, I thought of you, and could almost taste the sweetness of your kiss upon my lips.
Then yesterday became today, and you were there.
Your mouth spoke words of sweetness and love, and I was drawn to you,
I held you close, and kissed you gently, and the dream was again reality.
A fleeting moment, a tender kiss, the warmth of one to another,
And I loved you as the wind played upon your face.

Yesterday I thought of you, and wished you here beside me through the long dark night,
Then yesterday became today, and you are here.
And as you gently rest your head upon the pillow close to mine,
I shall join you in your softest dreams, I shall hold you close and safe.
And when the morning comes, and my eyes open to greet the day,
I shall think of you, turn, and you'll still be here. . .

Parting Words

And so, I bring to an end *Aztecs and Conquistadors*. To those who have taken the time to read this collection I can only say, "Muchas gracias y adios amigos."

Dear reader,

We hope you enjoyed reading *Of Aztecs and Conquistadors*. Please take a moment to leave a review, even if it's a short one. Your opinion is important to us.

Discover more books by Juan Pablo Jalisco at https://www.nextchapter.pub/authors/brian-porter-mystery-author-liverpool-united-kingdom

Want to know when one of our books is free or discounted? Join the newsletter at http://eepurl.com/bqqB3H

Best regards,
Juan Pablo Jalisco and the Next Chapter Team

Of Aztecs and Conquistadors
ISBN: 978-4-86751-767-3 (Large Print)

Published by
Next Chapter
1-60-20 Minami-Otsuka
170-0005 Toshima-Ku, Tokyo
+818035793528
20th July 2021

Lightning Source UK Ltd.
Milton Keynes UK
UKHW010644020821
388172UK00003B/504